VIP SECRETS FOR THE FREQUENT FLYER

HOW TO TRAVEL FIVE-STAR ON A THREE-STAR BUDGET

★ ★ ★ ★ ★

YOUR MUST HAVE TRAVEL GUIDE
TO ENJOY THE JOURNEY

A Guide For The Business or Pleasure Traveler

GINA DAGOSTINO

#1 National Best Selling Author

VIP Guide for the Frequent Flyer

#1 Best Selling Author

VIP Guide for the Frequent Flyer

How to Travel Five-Star on a Three-Star Budget

By Gina Dagostino

"Twenty years from now you will be more disappointed by the things you didn't do than by the ones you did do. So throw off the bowlines. Sail away from the safe harbor. Catch the trade winds in your sails. Explore. Dream. Discover."

-Mark Twain

Learn how to maximize your travel expense account, receive more coaching, travel tips, tricks and additional information at:

www.CreativeConsultingNetwork.com

www.HowToTravelFiveStar.com

Join our Facebook community and share your stories with us!

https://www.facebook.com/traveltvshow

Limits of Liability and Disclaimer of Warranty

The author and publisher shall not be liable for your misuse of this material. This book is strictly for informational and educational purposes.

Disclaimer

The views expressed are those of the author and do not reflect the official policy or position of any mentioned corporations, privately owned businesses, websites, persons or places cited in this publication.

Copyright © 2017 by CreativeConsultingNetwork.com

Table of Contents

Endorsements ix
Dedication xi
Note from the Author… xiii
Why Did I Write This Book? 1
Chapter 1. Discovery 5
Chapter 2. Fear not frequent flyer 9
Chapter 3. Security 19
Chapter 4. Credit can't buy me love 23
Chapter 5. So many choices 31
Chapter 6. I have Arrived! (now what?) 51
Chapter 7. Oh to rest my Weary Head 61
Chapter 8. To Uber or not to Uber 67
Chapter 9. Jet Setting 75
Chapter 10. Final Thoughts 81
About the Author 83

Endorsements and Accolades

"The information provided in this book and coaching sessions have made my corporate travel life much more stress-free, comfortable. As a result, I'm creating more productivity on work/travel days. Traveling two or more times per month can be very taxing on your mind and body. These are tips everyone should be privy to. You only know this information by doing it. I'm so glad to be following these simple guidelines. I'm happier and so are my co-workers."

> — Darron Guinn, Research and Development and Sales Leadership Manager of CSM Global Bakery Products.

"These ideas are so simple, yet the strategies are brilliant to maintain a first-class experience every time you fly. Just follow these guidelines to get the most from your journey. I'm so happy I read this book. I travel now with ease knowing I've gotten the best bang for my buck!!"

> — Mark D'Agostino, CFO Community Resources, Staten-Island, NY.

Dedication

Thank you to Mike Koenigs and Ed Rush for making this dream a reality. They are truly my mentors and lifeline for making this book journey possible.

Note from the Author...

It's lonely at the top.
NO, it isn't.
In actuality, it's lonely in the *middle*.

This book is for all to enjoy, but it's particularly dedicated to those, like me, who were a middle child. Just because you were a middle child does not mean you have to end up in a middle seat. Nor does it mean you have to end up middle class, middle of the road, caught in the middle, or afraid of middle age because you never really did what you set out to accomplish. You may have been a middle child, but don't settle for being a middle adult. I **challenge** you to start TODAY, one small journey at a time, accomplishing steps toward making your dreams a reality.

Although I have endless opportunities yet to explore, this book and my store, Uber Fun Factory, (Uberfunfactory.lol) are the beginning of this epic, five-star journey that I want to share with you! Being a middle child at middle age can sometimes be the BEST thing to happen to you.

Middle children hold specific elements of continuity that are undeniable. These experiences help you reach amazing heights while overcoming obstacles naturally because of the inevitable factors of always seeing the oldest getting praised and the youngest get coddled every moment of your young life. You're an ADULT now. Time to rise above up and have your own moments that are built on your epic adventures!

This is how I can take my story of being in the middle most of my life and connect the dots while making this travel guide, which is the crux of my inspiration to help one and all have FUN in their lives no matter what the circumstance. *VIP Guide for the Frequent Flyer* is for sale in my online store that I lovingly call Uber Fun Factory. If you travel but dislike your job, have fun with the journey. If you need to spice up your life in ANY respect be it large or small, find a way to make that journey fun. I am determined with all my heart to bring even just a little joy into your heart, while paying it forward, bringing joy into someone else's heart. This could be something as simple as a few nice words to the stranger you sat next to in the airport lounge or by giving a uniquely fun gift to a friend or loved one for no particular reason.

Note from the Author…

Come with me on my journey as I share some travel secrets with you. Then, visit my store Uberfunfactory.lol for some fun and inspiration. If I can bring a smile, a laugh, or some joy into your heart during this journey, it will make mine worthwhile. Fun is only fun if it's reciprocated. Thank you for receiving this book and my message to spread some joy. Now… Let's have some FUN and have an Epic-Five Star Journey. See you on the inside!

Please follow and like our social media travel pages on Facebook:

The Travel Channel@traveltvshow (https://www.facebook.com/traveltvshow/)

How to Travel Five Star@fivestarjourney (https://www.facebook.com/FiveStarJourney/)

Please visit our online fun store:

UberFunFactory.lol

Find this book:

http://www.clkmg.com/ginadag/1ygqn9

Why Did I Write This Book?

Forever safe, forever free. Let the wings of life take you where you're longing to be.

I love helping people in anyway that I can. What better way to help people than with something I love to do most...travel?! I have prepared this guide for you to take the pain out of getting to your destination: the stress of the journey, long lines, getting squashed in a middle seat, just to name a few. If you have experienced any of these common travel frustrations, keep reading; you are in for tips and tricks to solve these stresses and more.

Come with me - ride and fly with me as we go through U.S. travel in sequence, from booking the flight, hotel, car rental, to finding airport parking, to getting the most out of your travel with smart tricks at the airport and hotel. In sequence, *VIP Guide for the Frequent Flyer* provides all the things that need to be done, including scheduling travel, actually traveling, what to do at the airport, getting your rental car, and getting to your hotel.

I want everyone to enjoy their journey, whether for business or pleasure. I view my work as a pleasure. Use the information in this guide to prepare yourself for a level of comfort not already available or to prepare for a great adventure. I am not getting any kickbacks for my suggestions, nor do I have any affiliate marketing deals with any airlines or services that I use. I use them because they work. Feel safe knowing I've been there, done that. Of all the journeys I've taken, each has been the best journey I've been on yet!

In a general sense, this book will give you insights to make your travel days for work or pleasure stress-free, leaving you feeling confident, refreshed, and feeling like a first-class traveler.

This book will specifically take you through simple processes and steps to maximize your expense account or travel budget. You will receive step-by-step instructions on everything from saving money parking your car at the airport to getting the cheapest rate on your rental car, so you

Why Did I Write This Book?

have more money to play with for obtaining extra flight perks that will make flying the most exciting and relaxing part of your travel.

My travel days have now become just as important, and as much fun, as my vacation or work days. If I am working, I arrive at my work location refreshed and ready to go. I am able to get club access, so I can relax between flights - and I get the "best seat in the house" (on the plane) to travel in style and comfort.

See for yourself. There is something for everyone in this book. Even if you are aware of some of the things I cover here, there is sure to be much more that will help you in this "How to" Guide. This is the only travel guide you will ever need.

Whether you travel for work or play, weekly or once a year, there is a hidden gem in here just for you. Although I cater to the frequent flyer, there is something in this book for all who travel.

The exciting and rewarding world of travel awaits, and there are more travel tips, resources, and checklists to ensure you travel in style. Once you've read *VIP Guide for the Frequent Flyer*, don't forget to access the **VIP Bonus Travel Tips** by visiting www.HowToTravelFiveStar.com. Let the journey begin!

CHAPTER 1

Discovery

"The world is a book, and those who do not travel read only a page."

\- Saint Augustine

Whether you are traveling for work or pleasure, this chapter applies to everyone. Because of my own personal travel throughout the years for work and play, the people alone that you meet can create lasting impressions. That is something you will always have and hold in your treasure box. I'm a photographer, please trust me when I say, there is so much to see. Honor the experience by documenting its beauty with your camera. Capture it all.

VIP Guide for the Frequent Flyer

Even when you travel for work, there are places you can find to mingle with the locals, and really get a feel for the city you are in. I highly recommend when on business travel, you get out there and have a night or two on your own, without the business dinner pressures, and get into the local atmosphere of the town. Small talk even in small towns can turn into big revelations.

More astounding to me is the number of people I have met who have never actually even been on a plane. I can't fathom that. If you're reading this book, maybe you can't either. What is the relevance of a life where you stay in one place, and interact with the same people, day after day, year after year? I learned early I wanted a wider field of vision for my day-to-day life.

My first big travel journey was moving from a little town in upstate New York all the way to Los Angeles, California when I was twenty-one. Granted, although I drove, it opened up my heart and my mind to a whole new world. The cultural superfluity forces you to see things in an entirely new light. It took a few years, but I absconded from my small town way of thinking and grew into a

Chapter 1 - Discovery

whole new person, full of ideas and an abundance of openness to everything around me. I feel blessed and grateful to have been freed from the potential chains that bind many of those willing only to experience one page in the book of life.

I want to inspire those who don't travel to get out, take flight, and discover more about themselves in the process. I would like to incite action in those who travel for work frequently, to get out there and experience the "what" of "where" you are. Make it just a little less like work, and for those of you traveling for fun, give a pointer or two about enhancing your travel experience.

CHAPTER 2

Fear Not Frequent Flyer

"We can easily forgive a child who is afraid of the dark; the real tragedy of life is when men (or women) are afraid of the light."

- Plato

You might be surprised to read I had a huge fear of flying years ago that impeded my ability to take the leap and see the world. My thirst for adventure, and the strategy involved in pulling it off with ease, hungered for attention. What got me over my fear of flying? I was lucky enough once to sit next to a pilot who happened to be traveling as a passenger, probably to get him back home, or to another destination to man a flight. Why was this lucky? Well, I was worrying, "Why are we slowing down? Why are we speeding up? Why are we making such an abrupt turn? What's that noise?" The list could go on and on. I know I drove the pilot crazy asking him every question that popped into my head, due to a change in speed, altitude, or angle. However, this opportunity cured me for life. It pushed aside all my fears of flying because I became knowledgeable about the how's and why's of flight. Little did I know how much the pilots are working during our journey. Suddenly, the quirky movements and odd sounds weren't fear inducing. It all made sense now. The pilots were just following commands from air traffic control to stay safe and on the best course, in relation to all the other planes in the air at that time.

Pre 9-11, United had a channel that allowed you to listen to air traffic control. At any given time, air traffic control would control three to five planes, inclusive of the one I was on. When I started to listen to the channel, it became great entertainment, as well as a learning tool to figure out the special *air lingo*. Eventually, I could predict what the plane would be doing after certain commands and figure out strategies of the sky, opening myself up to a whole new level of *secret knowledge*. It made me feel

Chapter 2 - Fear Not Frequent Flyer

somewhat like a spy, in a good way, of course. Here I was, suddenly someone who was privy to this other world of information, and with the ability to decode it.

The first thing was always to figure out which pilot out of the bunch on that channel was our plane. Once I got that figured out, which was fun in and of itself, it was easy to follow the conversation. While flying across the country, the pilot was passed quite a few times from tower to tower, to continue the journey as instructed with a smooth transition from air traffic controller to air traffic controller.

What astounded me, even more, was the amount of communication necessary to deliver us safely across the skies. Contact with Air Traffic Control is crucial to being a pilot and demands constant attention. They are *on the job* for every second of that flight. So any thoughts I had about the pilot being on auto-pilot while I worried about what was going wrong between my seat-side cocktails were allayed immediately. This is me talking, the girl who was afraid to fly and let my dreams of the world live only in my rural community. Now, I fly all the time. Cross country trips just for a one-day stay, flying last minute for an opportunity to see some crazy event. Whatever the occasion, you get over the insecurities flying can evoke quickly when you do it all the time. It becomes just a natural part of your day, like driving a car is for many.

Statistically speaking, you are more likely to get hurt, severely injured, or killed in a car accident. The statistics on that are clear. According to *USA Today:*

> The National Safety Council compiled an odds-of-dying table for 2008, which further illustrates the relative risks of flying, and driving safety. It calculated the odds of dying in a motor vehicle accident to be one in ninety-eight for a lifetime. For air, and space transport (including air taxis, and private flights), the odds were one in seven thousand, one hundred, seventy-eight for a lifetime, according to the table.[1]

---

[1] "Is Air Travel Safer Than Car Travel?" *USA Today*. Gannett. Web. <http://traveltips.usatoday.com/air-travel-safer-car-travel-1581.html>

Chapter 2 - Fear Not Frequent Flyer

If anything, the stats have only improved with time, so, if your fear of flying is preventing you from climbing on board with me and learning my time-saving travel tips, you're missing an exciting world out there. The scariest thing you can do with your time is waste it, or be held prisoner to your own fears, and insecurities.

More times than not, flying is not for the vacationer. Rather, it's for the opportunist; the person who can dare to travel to where the opportunities are, because they aren't going to fall in your lap.

Read on, enjoy the journey, and have safe and fun travels because of this. Live a happier and fuller life, and be more productive. I'll hold your hand while we take off.

This book is a culmination of information I have gathered over years of flying myself, arranging flights for others, and using travel services of all kinds. My intent is to make this as systematic for you as it is for me.

In no time at all, you will discover that you are the super sleuth who can arrange your own travel itineraries utilizing all the tips, tricks, and resources I will give you. You too will have great satisfaction in knowing you got your entire trip - not only for the best price - but also for the highest comfort level possible.

So, put those seat belts on and tray tables up. Sit back, and enjoy the journey.

This book is going to walk you all the way through a travel process. From parking your car at the airport to finally resting your head on that pillow. Let's start with something as simple as airport parking.

This can be something you just go and do and pay an outrageous full price, or you can spend fifteen extra minutes on this before you go and save a significant amount of money while getting the royal treatment. For all the cities I have traveled in and out of, with large and smaller international airports, there is always a parking deal to be had. Many of them are off-site and unrelated to the airport, so many miss a great opportunity to save money and have peace of mind by not looking into it for themselves.

Chapter 2 - Fear Not Frequent Flyer

For instance, if you are traveling from southern California, you have several options for airports and more than enough options for safe parking. Los Angeles International Airport (LAX) is the largest airport that flies anywhere, and everywhere, without multiple connections. Burbank International is not far from LAX, but is much easier to navigate around, with less chance of being in the wrong terminal at the wrong time. Ontario International Airport, about an hour inland from there, is small and easy to navigate through and much less stressful, all things considered. Because of its locale, you may have more connections than you want, depending on the destination. There can be some lengthy layovers when using small airports, so keep this in mind.

When you Google search **cheap airport parking near...** (and name your airport), you will usually have some options. Some will be situated at a hotel with a shuttle service, others will be a privately owned parking structure. But you can always find cheaper than airport parking. I found one at each of the airports I use as my main hubs. Not only is the parking inexpensive, but they actually let you

VIP Guide for the Frequent Flyer

drop off your bags and car at the door for the valet to take care of. You just hop into their shuttle van. In the case of Ontario International Airport, the shuttle comes around directly to pick-up points near your vehicle once you've parked it yourself.

I would call this five-star service. You don't have to drive miles to find a spot, or arrive super early, only to get out of your car, drag your bags half a football field to the bus stop where you…wait…then wait some more…then perhaps, if you're lucky, not start the trip already stressed. Why worry you're going to be late, only to arrive with an aching back and a pressing need to find the closest chiropractor once you reach your destination?

It is worth the few extra minutes online after you have booked your trip. Most of these parking places allow you to make a reservation, which you aren't paying for in advance, in case something changes last minute. Groupon carries discounts for some parking places as well.

In every step of the journey, you look for the best service for the price. That takes a little bit of super-sleuthing, but it's fun when you achieve your

Chapter 2 - Fear Not Frequent Flyer

result. Once you get used to it, it becomes second nature, or you can utilize the same services without having to re-investigate in certain areas, like parking at your home based airport.

You would think, something like parking at the airport is a no-brainer. However, there are opportunities to save money and have five-star service. Personally, I use "The Park" at LAX (no affiliation here), which is less than five dollars a day with advanced reservation, and parking at the front door, hopping right into the shuttle van. They park your car for you, and when you return, the driver from the shuttle calls with your ticket number, so your car is waiting for you at the front when you are home.

Not every city has services this good, but many are close in rank. So do your homework. Make the most of your travel dollar. It's your hard earned money (or the company's you want to save for your flight). Wouldn't you rather put the money you save toward something else on your journey more exciting than parking?

For more parking resources, access your copy of **VIP Bonus Travel Tips** by visiting www.HowToTravelFiveStar.com. Don't let the cost of parking limit your VIP experience!

CHAPTER 3

Security

*"If you want total security, go to prison.
There you're fed, clothed, given medical care and so on.
The only thing lacking...is freedom."*

- Dwight D. Eisenhower

This chapter by itself will save you so much time, anxiety, and relieve travel stress for you, which is my ultimate goal. Once we get this out of the way, the rest will be super easy. You may not even be aware that TSA offers a pre-check service you can register for that allows for quicker turns through the security line.

My first experience with TSA pre-check was during their initial phase. At random, I had been selected to try this unique line. Huh? I don't need to take my liquids or my laptop out? I can keep my shoes on? This constitutes a *line?* Wow! I was excited! Going through security just like back in the old days. But how? Why? Well, that is exactly what TSA was trying to get people to ask. TSA Pre-check line: the great new way to go through security with less hassle, stress, and more quality time to relax, get some work done or have something to eat. What a concept. I love this idea. But it must be expensive? A new government money-maker?

To my surprise, it was quite the opposite. It's only $85, and it covers you for five years. Talk about a five-star treatment you can take to the bank. This line is short and stress-free.

How many times have you gone through airport security at six a.m. or five p.m. to find the lines extremely long? On top of that, having the daunting task of removing practically all your clothing, and unpacking your carry-on and personal items that you just spent time tediously packing so you can quickly access everything, only to find its contents strewn over gray security tubs, and the rest on the belt going through the x-ray machine?

Chapter 3 - Security

If you have ever at this moment asked yourself the following questions in your head, you're not alone. Am I the only person with so much *stuff* that I have to remove from myself and my bags? Why does it seem like I'm the only one holding up the line? Will I make it past the body scanner before my *stuff*? What if someone swipes my computer while I'm in the line to go through the body scanner? Can that scanner really see you naked?

What is the process of TSA Pre-check? TSA is a government run department that is part of Homeland Security. This is a three step process. In the first step, you file an application online, and make your appointment to go to your nearest TSA office. Mind you, for those that travel a lot make an appointment to go to the TSA office in whatever city you will be in during their available calendar days. Appointments can be as much as far as four weeks out, so this is why I recommend starting this process first. At the appointment, you show two forms of ID and get your fingerprints done. The third step involves a thorough search of records by the department of homeland security for any criminal history. This takes some time to complete.

In total, I would give TSA about eight weeks from the date your application is received to assign you a pre-check number.

Learn more about TSA and other time-saving travel programs by accessing **VIP Bonus Travel Tips** at www.HowToTravelFiveStar.com. Do yourself a favor and take the one major step in travel that is going to save you the most heartache!

CHAPTER 4

Credit Can't Buy Me Love

"...But it can get you access to the business clubs and get you closer to those upgrades and free trips."

- Gina Dagostino

It was Christmas time, and I was in New York flying back to California. I had thoroughly exhausted myself, I was sick, (thank goodness the Ebola outbreak wasn't in the news yet, or I would not have been allowed on the plane!) and there was a massive storm about to hit the airport I was heading to. Christmas is a bad time to travel if you are not taking advantage of my recommendations. Airports are crowded, and some hubs get shut down due to weather. I was never happier in my life to have a United Club Pass than I was on this particular trip in 2013. As I was walking through the airport, the lines were ridiculously long at customer service, and flights (including my connection) were being canceled. I came to my senses, and remembered the club card in my wallet. I walked into that club, and there were two greeters to assist me with my travel dilemma. No line. Fantastic! Five-Star service that was more than I expected. The goal was to get out of that city before the storm hit and find connections back to Los Angeles that weren't canceled. They were able to do this, three times over, to ensure the best possibility of making it home.

As I planted myself in a little corner getting much-needed rest, these gals at the desk came to me three to four times with alternatives that were being updated as quickly as the storm was changing. Who knew how the flight status was going to change next? (Not only that, my luggage arrived with all those changes on the plane in which I was flying.) Did I make it home on time? Yes, I certainly did. Did I have an ounce of stress because of the lines

Chapter 4 - Credit Can't Buy Me Love

outside the club? Not even. Did this airline club perk save my trip from being a complete disaster?

Would you be surprised to know I may have had to spend a few days sleeping in the airport without a change of clothes? Would you be more surprised to know I didn't? Yes. They put their best service-minded people at the helm in these clubs to cater to those of us who have a certain expectation. Talk about the best investment I ever made in my life!

Do I use my United Club Pass often? No. Frankly, I prefer being out in the natural habitat of the airport talking to random people and hearing their stories rather than sitting in a room with very few exits. But for those times you do really need the services that give you great peace of mind? Priceless. There are times when you absolutely need the services of the club. So, how do you get this service?

You can pay $50 a pop every time you go in; however, in the grand scheme of things, you probably need (vs. want) their services twice a year, so for a mere hundred dollars for the year,

VIP Guide for the Frequent Flyer

you'd be doing alright. Remember to bring the card with you on travel day. If you're a frequent flyer, it's probably tucked away in your wallet the way it should be.

You can enroll in the United Mileage Plus card program and pay $95 for one year's membership. You'll get two free club passes, and many perks worth the time of adding your name to the list of members they service. You can earn two dollars per mile when booking your flight and/or car rentals. Your first checked bag is free (saving $35 each time you fly). You also get an upgrade to *boarding group 2* (another five-star perk), so you can get on the plane early. You are virtually guaranteed to have the space you need in the overhead luggage bin and the chance to get settled into your extra legroom seat. Even if you fly only three times in one year, you will get a return on your credit card investment from the checked bag fee alone. With all the additional perks you get, it's well worth the small yearly fee.

Under what other circumstances might I need the club if I am not a business traveler? If you are

Chapter 4 - Credit Can't Buy Me Love

on that trip to just outright get there and save all the money you possibly can, having the club as a perk can help you in your endeavor of having a truly free trip. If you happen to have more of a layover than you want because you got a great trip booked for only 12,500 miles each way, then use your club card. Food and drinks inside the club are complimentary, and you do have a gorgeous space to relax, catch up on work, charge up all your devices without fighting the crowds for charging stations like it's a Black Friday item.

Am I getting any paid advertising from United? No. Then why am I using them as an example? Because it's the card and the airline I use. I like to stick with that I know. It has all the perks that I need, including free club access, to make my overall travel experience a five-star experience every time.

So what is my suggestion? It's pretty simple. First, you must be a responsible credit card user. Then buy your large purchases (that you have the cash for) on it. I put a down payment for my car on it, and received three-thousand miles from a down payment I was going to pay with cash anyway. So,

I paid my credit card instead of the vendor. The more you can do that, the more you will accumulate those precious miles that will allow you free flights and upgrades to first class.

What now? Spend some time doing your homework, and you will have the information you need for all the times you travel. The idea is for travel to become systematic. Which airline do you fly with the most? If you have one, and are responsible with credit, get their credit card. If you use different carriers all the time equally, then either sign up for your favorite airline's card, or go with AMEX, which can apply your mileage to any air carrier. That may be the best way to go if you don't need other perks specific to one airline, like club passes. Either way, I can't stress enough the importance of paying your credit card in full every month. If you're going into debt to save money on travel, then what's the point? Have a good heart to heart with yourself about the reality of you being a responsible card user, or having someone you are accountable to, if needed, so that you do keep your promise to yourself.

Chapter 5 - So Many Choices…

If you want to save even more time (because time IS money), access your copy of **VIP Bonus Travel Tips** by visiting www.HowToTravelFiveStar.com.

CHAPTER 5

So Many Choices…

*"The choices we make lead up to actual experiences.
It is one thing to decide to climb a mountain.
It is quite another to be on top of it."*

- Herbert A. Simon

Whether traveling for business or pleasure, whether deciding to travel at all, and how- -by land, sea, or air, we are paving the path for possible unusual life experiences we could have never foreseen. The fun thing about travel is that with every choice you make, every step of the way, your experience will be completely different had you chosen a different seat, a different flight, or a different airline. The paths with whom you cross, the conversations you'll have or not have, the magazine you happen to pick up, the place you buy your coffee or water, it's all a story waiting to be created. So create your journey, and consider these factors in the choices you make. It will change your perspective on the process and put you in a different mindset when making your trip.

Which airline do I choose for my trip? How do I find the best deal, save the extra money, and use these savings wisely when booking my flight to get the most comfortable seat possible? These are all frequently asked questions that vary slightly from destination to destination.

Let's begin with choosing an airline. Choosing an airline, especially for the business traveler, is going to depend on your destinations. First, you must ask yourself, are you flying to the same two or three destinations most of the year for business? If so, it's worth it, in the long run, to pay more money for some flights as long as you stay consistent with the same airlines.

By utilizing the same airlines, you are gaining coveted miles as well as building your status toward complimentary upgrades and five-star treatment by getting into platinum lines and priority baggage handling. In other words, you may fly enough that

Chapter 5 - So Many Choices...

you reach platinum or gold status. If you have paid slightly more for coach on a cross-country flight, you automatically get bumped up to first class twenty-four – forty-eight hours before you leave because of your status. Isn't that worth the comfort and convenience of paying that extra money? If you were to buy a first class ticket across the country, round trip, you would pay minimally $1,100 – $1,500 on average. If you were a frequent flyer and had to pay $650 – $800 for a last minute booking, but get upgraded using miles, or better yet for free using your status with the airlines, wouldn't that be worth it?

If you are not sure yet, think of the money you are saving in other areas that make up this difference in your budget ($40 in airport parking, $200 on a rental car, $300 or more on a hotel). That more than makes up for the extra money you will pay for a flight to get better seats, even if you simply pay for extra legroom economy and know which seats are the best choice.

Back to the question: Which airline? There is a simple system I use which has proved time and again to never fail. Keep in mind, I have no affiliations of any kind with the sources I am mentioning. It's just my method; it's what I do. My first step in choosing an airline is to go to two travel sites and compare them. The first one is Kayak.com. Why do I choose this one? Well, this is more of a true to scale, accurate tell-all resource. Kayak doesn't offer discounts, but they compare MOST (keyword) major airlines. What does this do? Well, it allows you to get an overall scope of what's happening with flights and fares during your travel period.

Step two in this process is to go to a discount airline website, such as Travelocity, Priceline, or whoever you like best on a premium site. What does this allow you to do? This will then give you an idea of the airlines offering the lowest rates and discounted price points.

Why compare the two, and why not buy from either of those sites directly? I have found in most instances, after that research, by then going directly to the one or two airline websites directly that offer good prices, you may find a cheaper flight than even those on offer with the discount site. If the price is the same, you are better off still booking directly with the airline. There are fewer hassles that way,

Chapter 5 - So Many Choices…

and you are gathering precious points to use later. Some discounted sites will not allow you to collect miles for your flight, even if you are a member of that airline.

There is another reason, however, in utilizing this method. Southwest is not affiliated with any of these websites. Many times, if you are booking in advance, you will find that by far, Southwest Airlines has the best rates for their "wanna get away?" fares. As well, there are many superior advantages to Southwest Airlines over all the others. Let's go over that list.

This is all practical knowledge and experience from years of flying. Southwest has the best policy if you do not use their ticket. First of all, there is no change fee. This is a huge perk. If you don't use a ticket on any other airlines, their change fee plus the difference in the fair is like paying for another ticket. Changes do not come cheap. This is something that could put you in the negative financially for your trip.

We all know things happen, and life can get in the way, especially when you book a trip very far in advance, or for your job. The advantage is you get great rates, but the disadvantage is those high rates go right out the window if something comes up last minute that doesn't allow you to leave when expected.

Southwest is not a fancy airline; there is no upgrading to extra legroom seats or to first class. However, the bulkhead and the exit rows have plenty of legroom. As well, on both sides of the plane, there is an exit row seat with a seat missing in front of it. That gives you tons of extra room. My clients who are over six feet tall really appreciate this knowledge. As well, there are no baggage surcharges if you have two bags that are within the size parameters and airline's weight limit (fifty pounds). Overall, not having a first class and paying their baggage fees, in the long run, saves you the hassle and expense of knowing you have those choices.

The great thing about Southwest is that all their airplanes are Boeing series 737's. That means consistency in-plane configuration, and no issues with having a carry-on that won't fit in the overhead bin because the small jet, or prop commuter plane, is your only option for the route you are taking.

Chapter 5 - So Many Choices...

Here is the great Southwest secret. They board, as most of you know, in groups "A," "B" and "C." It may seem a mystery as to how to get into the "A" group, which gives you the best option for seat choices and availability of overhead carry-on space.

This can be your best friend. There are three ways you can get into the "A" group. The first one takes a commitment to get online, ready to check in, and get your boarding pass exactly twenty-four hours (Not one hour after. Not twenty minutes after. At exactly the twenty-four-hour mark before your flight.) The secret to getting in the "A" group is timing. They go by who checks in, in what order. If you want to set calendars and alarms and make sure you are available at this exact moment, I can almost guarantee you will get into the "A" group. (As a side note, you will not be stuck in a middle seat if you are B32 or higher). If you are not interested in this approach, try the following.

A better way, during the checkout process, is to pay an extra $15 each way to have the computers automatically check you in. Therefore, you are checked in forty-eight hours in advance. This means Business Select passengers automatically get A1-

A15. Early Bird checks ins (pay the fifteen dollars) get any A's after that. However, there was once a flight I booked onto that was super busy and had many early bird payers, therefore, I still ended up with a "B" boarding number. This is still a good number if you don't have a particular seat you want to make a beeline for.

However, there is still a third way you can beat this system and end up being one of the first to board while you are at the gate. Sometimes, I save the $30 in early bird check-in and pay at the gate between $30 - $40 per flight segment to get upgraded to first class. The closest thing to first class on a Southwest flight is Business Select. This means you are one of the first fifteen passengers to board, which gives you a great chance at getting that coveted exit row seat or bulkhead--you also get a free drink ticket or two.[2]

Here is what I look at when I am deciding on whether to upgrade. How long are my flight segments, and how much time do I have in between

---

[2] "Boarding the Plane - Travel Experience - Southwest Airlines." *Boarding the Plane - Travel Experience - Southwest Airlines.* Web. <https://www.southwest.com/html/travel-experience/boarding-your-flight/>

Chapter 5 - So Many Choices…

flight segments? That way, if my first flight is lengthy, and I have a quick connection, I am going to want to upgrade, get a comfortable seat, and potentially sit in a bulkhead vs. the exit row so that I can be the first to exit the plane. I want to give myself every chance of getting to my next gate on time so that I don't miss the connection or my place in line for a great seat.

Many times, if I have to book a trip last minute, it used to make me think, *"I'm screwed, this is going to cost a fortune."* Well, let me share with you what I do in these instances that can make a trip the most economical while giving you a first class experience. Keep in mind that we are saving in other areas of our journey so that we can utilize those dollars wisely for an excellent flight experience. Let's look at three scenarios for flying on a trip across country from LAX (Los Angeles, CA) to EWR (Newark, one of New York City's airports.) The three scenarios are #1 - paying outright for the ticket, #2 - paying for the ticket and using mileage to upgrade to first class, or #3 - using just miles for your trip.

My two airlines of choice, unless there is a special circumstance, are United and Southwest. If I have

VIP Guide for the Frequent Flyer

to book a trip last minute (and sometimes even if I don't), it best suits my needs to book two one way tickets. However, it's good to always check round-trip prices against two one ways on two different airlines. One-way tickets used to be more expensive than a round trip. Keep in mind, costs with airlines are always changing. Even if it's not cheaper on two one ways, my hope is if you get into the habit of doing the homework yourself, you will reap the money saving benefits. In utilizing my airline miles for United, they have different amounts of mileage for various tiers of travel.

Here is a rough chart of the paid one-way ticket choices on an outbound from LAX to New York.

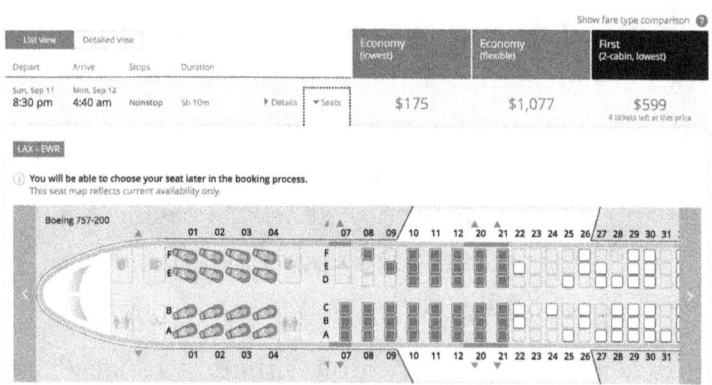

(www.united.com)

Chapter 5 - So Many Choices...

The choices are quite favorable. You have an incredibly inexpensive economy class for $175. To which you could spend an extra $125 for a very comfortable upgraded economy seat in the second exit row with power outlets, free entertainment, and the limited recline by the exit seat in front of you (and you are full recline) which gives you a ton of space. With your United plus mileage card, you board second after first class, and your first checked bag is free. Getting quickly through this busy airport in the TSA line makes this a favorable option, especially if you're flying at peak hours. Alternatively, you could fly first class for $600, which is a great deal. Notice in the screenshot above that first class is business class.

Business class has sleeper seats (fully recline like sleeping in a bed), privacy, outlets, free meals, and all you care to drink if you are using a cab or Uber on the other side. It is very comfortable. There is no waiting in line at the ticket counter to check in. Two bags are free, you get through security in the first class line, board first, get a drink before you take off, and receive a menu for your meal. Relax. Watch movies, TV shows or, listen to music. There is also plenty of space to get work done, and no waiting for the first class restroom.

If you add up the hard costs, your one hundred seventy-five dollars spent on a cheap ticket can quickly add up to nearly the same cost. Let's do the math.

- Ticket = $175
- Upgrade = $135
- 1st luggage = $35
- 2nd luggage = $45
- Food & drink = $30

It may make you feel better that you got your ticket for only one hundred seventy-five dollars, but realistically, you may want the complete stress-free comfort of traveling business class. As I said, we will save enough in other areas to cover this.

Let's look at scenario number 2.

Using miles to upgrade to first class while paying for a ticket. I have to admit that sometimes this is the worst option, however, at times, it's not. You will see this in a moment. Depending on the

Chapter 5 - So Many Choices...

circumstance, you will make the most favorable choice for your situation.

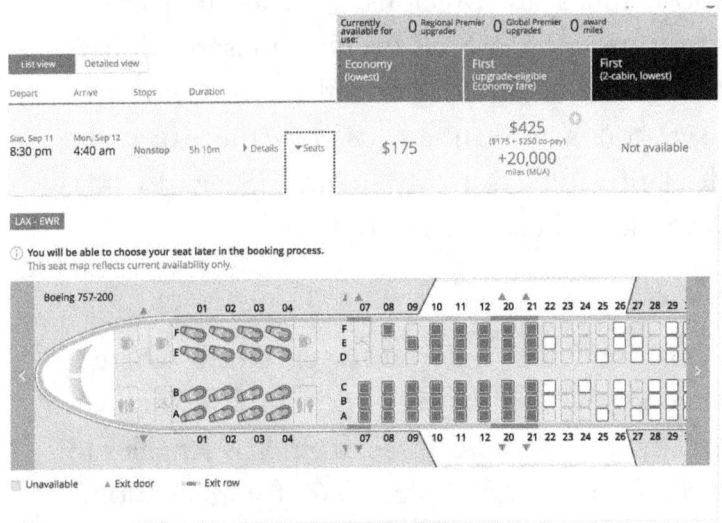

(www.united.com)

As you can see, you have the same choice of the $175 economy ticket, which all things considered, on a long flight like that, you will be spending in the neighborhood of $450. For a little less money, $425 plus 20,000 miles (which trust me, you will earn miles quickly), you can fly business class with all the luxuries and amenities stated earlier in this chapter. The only decision you need to make is whether it's worth spending the twenty-thousand miles, or paying an extra one hundred-fifty dollars outright for first class, instead of using your miles.

Those miles are precious. It takes two cross-country trips, or close to twenty-thousand dollars on your credit card, to recoup that. In having this mindset, you may want to just pay the extra one hundred fifty dollars to fly in first (Scenario #1). However, let's check our last option.

Scenario #3

Using only miles for your travel. This is where it gets interesting and the most economical for five-star treatment. As you can see, from Los Angeles to Newark, it's only 12,500 plus $5.60 for an economy seat. If you spend the $125-$135 to upgrade to 21A from 21F, you are sitting with more room than in first class, as this particular flight does not offer business class. They are "regular" first class seats. Comparatively, sometimes I think the exit rows have more room than first class. But that will be up to you to decide.

Remember from our miles plus money scenario, first class was 20,000 miles plus $430. In this scenario, for only 5,000 additional miles (twenty-five thousand

Chapter 5 - So Many Choices...

in total) and $5.60, you are in first class all the way. Of the three choices, which sounds the best to you? For me, I would take the twenty-five thousand miles--and get all the perks and benefits of first class for under six dollars (that's not a typo!). Keep in mind, with first class, no matter what, you skip the lines. Baggage, meals, drinks, and entertainment are free. That is my choice in this scenario.

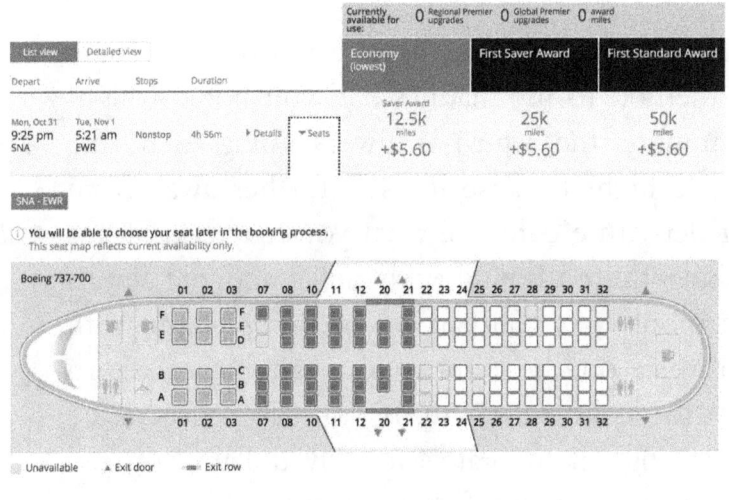

(www.united.com)

There are other times when they have a fully flexible economy fare or a first class fare for the same twenty-five thousand miles. So pay close attention when you are looking at these charts. Why would you waste twenty-five thousand miles to be squashed in economy, when you can sit in first class for the same amount of miles? Always get the most for your money and your miles. This is how you make your decisions in a relatively quick and practical way.

So, now that we are flying first class to New York for six dollars, let's check on the return.

I'm using Southwest for the return trip. There is a method to my madness. If you book a flight last minute, the return is always going to be the cheaper flight because it's still further away from your departure date. So, what you may consider is booking the outbound with miles and the return with money. As you can see in this scenario with Southwest on the return, you can buy a return ticket for as little as $140. If you use my secret of "upgrading" at the gate for forty dollars, you can choose your best comfortable seat for this trip.

Chapter 5 - So Many Choices...

All fares are rounded up to the nearest dollar.

Depart	Arrive	Flight #	Routing	Travel Time	Business Select $655	Anytime $627	Wanna Get Away $147 - $218
6:05 AM	10:55 AM	28 / 3218	1 stop Change Planes DEN	7h 50m	$655	$627	$197
6:15 AM	10:55 AM	1540 / 2671	1 stop Change Planes MDW	7h 40m	$655	$627	$218
9:50 AM	3:40 PM	1551 / 1969	1 stop Change Planes MDW	8h 50m	$655	$627	$197
12:45 PM	5:30 PM	1334 / 1849	1 stop Change Planes PHX	7h 45m	$655	$627	$197
3:35 PM	8:00 PM	1553 / 286	1 stop Change Planes MDW	7h 25m	$655	$627	$183
4:35 PM	9:25 PM	381 / 474	1 stop Change Planes LAS	7h 50m	$655	$627	$197
5:05 PM	10:15 PM	482 / 1599	1 stop Change Planes MDW	8h 10m	$655	$627	$183
5:40 PM	11:10 PM	1963 / 1571	1 stop Change Planes DEN	8h 30m	$655	$627	$147

(www.united.com)

So let's recap: one round-trip from Los Angeles to New York for a total of $187, and forfeiting twenty-five miles to get first class on the outbound trip, and business select on the way back. That is a significant savings and five-star treatment for a two-star price.

I don't know how much time you spend booking travel, but if you start with an hour to get the hang of it, it will become super routine. Already knowing what your favorite airlines are is a step towards being more efficient. Having your go-to airlines makes it so much easier.

I know it's not always possible, but when it is, stick to two airlines, and use them as your mainstay. It will help you get used to the system, get more miles, get better deals, seats, and treatment all faster.

This is a serious note worth mentioning. "Economy Class Syndrome" is real. Frequent flying can cause health problems, as can long flights all cramped up in an economy seat.[3] For you frequent corporate travelers, it may be worth your while to get a doctor's note to give to your superior giving you permission to upgrade automatically to at least the upgraded extra legroom economy class. I am channeling my previous nursing career when I say Deep Vein Thrombosis (DVT's) are no joke, not to mention the health risks to your neck, and lower back that over time may cause chronic pain. Talk to your expense account manager, and see if a simple thing such as a doctor's note can help you get to your destination feeling ready to go for that meeting, instead of ready to go to bed, or to a pile of paper to write a resignation notice. Now, onward travelers.

---

[3] "Definition of Economy Class Syndrome." *MedicineNet*. Web. <http://www.medicinenet.com/script/main/art.asp?articlekey=15872>

Chapter 5 - So Many Choices…

There's much more savings and first class treatment in store.

To learn even more airline and travel tips, access the **VIP Bonus Travel Tips** by visiting www.HowToTravelFiveStar.com.

CHAPTER 6

I have arrived! (Now what?)

"All you need is the plan, the roadmap, and the courage to press on to your destination."

- Earl Nightingale

("But it also helps to have a shuttle, Uber, town car or a rental car in place."

– Gina Dagostino)

I happen to love searching for a great deal with a rental car. This is truly the spot where you can save the most money, allowing you the extra funds for your flight perks. Depending on your expense account, and the loyalty program your company has, you may not have the luxury of shopping around, but it's because you get a great deal.

The joy in that is time management. You know the rental company, and with your profile and club card, you get first class treatment. When you are a frequent flier in the car rental sector, all you do is keep your information updated online (they only require credit card and driver's license information). Then all you do is go straight to a car. Yes, you heard me correctly. You don't sign in, you don't wait in line. Everything's done for you. Enterprise has an exceptional program where you can choose any car you want and just drive off into the sunset. With most other clubs, all you have to do is go to the kiosk outside where the cars are. They hand you the keys and point you to the car. No papers to sign or lines to wait in. There is usually a newspaper on the seat for you, as well.

If your company insists on using one particular company, don't fret. You can still at least try to book enough in advance that you can get the best deal possible. Being a frequent customer will get you better rates any day of the week, and collecting

Chapter 6 - I Have Arrived! (Now What?)

the miles will give you automatic upgrades to some cool cars.

Also, depending on why you are traveling, see if there is a shuttle to the hotel, or be the hero, and find out when others are traveling and carpool with them. You can save the company the cost of a rental, and have more money in the expense account for other trip perks--like dinners.

If you have the option of choosing a car rental company, then the research is somewhat the same as for the airlines. I compare Priceline, United, and Southwest for car rental prices, even if I am not flying with them. They tend to be very competitive. Recently, though, I have discovered a new site called carrentals.com. They have been the least expensive so far. But you can't stop there. There are two more alternatives when getting the absolute best price. If you love getting the best price, then complete these next two steps. It will be well worth it.

First, if and *only* if you have your travel dates and times set in stone, go to priceline.com and name your price for a car. Don't go with their suggested price. You already know from your research what the price range is. In this case, cut that daily rate by fifty percent, and start there. You won't get it the first time, but keep going up by twenty-five to fifty cents, and see who bites. In some cases, there are small rental car companies we haven't heard of that hide away in Raleigh, North Carolina, for instance, and happen to be called Advantage Choice car rental. In Albany, New York, you have Dollar and Alamo, aside from the big guys.

If you can't get the price you want through Priceline, I have a go-to where you can by-pass Priceline altogether, and get the best deal possible. That is by calling AAA and talking to someone in their travel department. Yes, you have to be a member of AAA to reap their rewards, but I can tell you nineteen out of twenty times, they had a better price than those on-line. You can join AAA for forty-eight dollars a year, but there are up-gradable versions that come with their own plentitude of exclusive benefits. Not to mention roadside assistance, towing, and bringing you gasoline if you ever need it. It's worth that small fee for all the savings you will enjoy. If you are using it for work travel purposes, check with your tax advisor about adding this to your yearly tax deductions. You may not know that AAA has a

Chapter 6 - I Have Arrived! (Now What?)

contract with Budget. Although nine times out of ten, Budget will be the best price, if they give you a price similar to those you have seen on-line, ask them if there is another car rental company with a lower price. There always will be.

Exception. The one and only time I came across an exception to this general rule that you can count on was when I went to North Carolina and discovered their secret small car rental company called Advantage Car Rental. When AAA couldn't beat any of the prices, I went to that company's website directly. What came up in Google was Advantage and this new site I found that I told you about: carrentals.com. Carrentals.com had the absolute best price for cars in that area at that time. I am not sure what was going on in that town the three days I was going to be there, but what started out as a potential car rental for $300 for two days, ended up costing me a total of $89 for both days. That saved me over $200! It took five minutes more online for my own super-sleuthing ways. I would have kicked myself to find out you could have gotten a car for less than the price of one day for both days. There was a lot of small-town charm and service as well.

VIP Guide for the Frequent Flyer

Reservation Details

Advantage Choice (or equivalent Special)

- Unlimited mileage
- Air Conditioning
- Automatic

Pick-up
Monday June 27th, 2016, 02:30 PM

CHARLOTTE - Douglas Airport (CLT)
5501 JOSH BIRMINGHAM PARKWAY
Charlotte, NC 28208

Drop-off
Wednesday June 29th, 2016, 06:00 AM

CHARLOTTE - Douglas Airport (CLT)
5501 JOSH BIRMINGHAM PARKWAY
Charlotte, NC 28208

Important informations
ADVANTAGE : IN TERMINAL - COUNTER

Contact information

Price Details

Car Rental

2 days @ USD 29.75 / day	USD 59.50
Estimated taxes & fees	USD 29.61
Total amount of your booking	USD 89.11

(https://www.advantage.com/reservations)

Chapter 6 - I Have Arrived! (Now What?)

Does this seem like too much work? Well, it's really not. 1) Go to United and Southwest.com under car rentals. See what the going rates are and note what the least expensive is. Then 2) call AAA and get the best rate possible, which is usually one-third to one-half the price. This is simple. If you are like me, and a bit OCD and wanting to make sure you get your upgraded seats on the plane, you will go the extra mile by trying Priceline, name your price. But don't forget, with that, you are committed to the purchase.

So don't lose your money if you think plans might change. AAA will be better because it's still just a reservation that does not get paid until you arrive. You can also use your frequent flyer number on the car rental or sign up for one. If you run into an unusual circumstance and have to do a little more detective work like I did in Raleigh to compare an obscure rental car company directly with it to carrentals.com, it can be well worth the time and savings.

That's the biggest consideration when using Priceline, or another offer, to prepay for your car to save a good chunk of money. Usually, in business travel, flexibility is a key component, but not always. So choose wisely. You will be thrilled at getting such a great deal.

In summary, car rental is the easiest and biggest savings you can land on your trip. Remember these two easy steps to save up to fifty percent. How awesome is that! It's all money you can put toward having a relaxing, stress-free flight. If you want to just go on the cheap, it's money in your pocket for spending on the trip or it can go back into your travel fund for upgrades.

Additionally, having AAA on your side is always a good thing. You never know what can happen, and having the security of AAA getting to you in thirty minutes or less if you are stranded away from home is a comfort you can't deny.

Happy driving everyone! I almost forgot, when you get to the counter, be polite and complimentary. It may get you an upgrade if you ask for it, especially if you are a club member. If you are like me, you will want the smaller car to save on gas. Just make sure the small car you are given has a trunk, not a hatch. You want to put your luggage in the trunk

Chapter 6 - I Have Arrived! (Now What?)

for safety in case you stop anywhere before getting to your hotel.

The best tip in this book is to not look like a tourist in your rental car. Thieves love it when you leave things in the open. Bags in the trunk and rental agreement and maps in the glove box when you park.

Get access to your copy of **VIP Bonus Travel Tips** at www.HowToTravelFiveStar.com for more transportation tips.

CHAPTER 7

Oh To Rest My Weary Head

"If you can dream it, you can do it."

- Walt Disney

A picture is worth a thousand words, but sometimes, even that isn't enough.

If the price of a hotel room is too good to be true, it probably is. I stayed in a no brand name boutique hotel in Hollywood some time ago. Everything in the hotel was updated. I am a stickler when it comes to being able to surmise what a hotel is like by the photographs. However, I was fooled this time. Everything was new and upgraded in the photos, but upon check in, the "dirt" on the hotel came through, and I am talking dirt and filth. White things, like towels and bedding, were

VIP Guide for the Frequent Flyer

now gray, there was a large wad of toothpaste on the bathroom door, and the sink counter had not been cleaned. It just wasn't clean. When I told the hotel manager about the roaches, they gave me a can of bug killer. Really? So how do you avoid this nightmare before you even get to sleep?

I wouldn't recommend AAA for this. I'm not sure how their grading system works, but it's hit or miss with hotel quality. Being on the road a lot, I find that there are two ways you can go. Straight up, Airbnb is a great money saver. Look at reviews, amenities, and location in reference to where you are spending most of your time. It's nice to have the roominess of a condo or house with full kitchen facilities if you are spending a week or more out of town.

I saved fifty percent by using Airbnb staying in a condo while in San Diego. The other way you can't go wrong is by using a hotel honors program. I am partial to the Hilton Honors program. They have a great selection of hotels and a good amount of rewards.

Chapter 7 - Oh To Rest My Weary Head

Personally, I find Hilton hotels to be very consistent and clean. All the hotels affiliated with the Hilton Honors program are exquisite hotels. Some rewards programs are about fifty-fifty in that aspect. If you are going to be staying anywhere in the US, you will always find a Hampton Inn, part of the Hilton Honors program. The rooms are large, have a refrigerator and microwave, amenities for working on the go, and they are consistent and clean. They also have a very nice hot breakfast from six a.m. to ten a.m. If you can drag yourself downstairs in time, it's a nice start to the day.

As far as their rewards point offers, Hampton offers a one night stay for points that add up quickly when you use them or their subsidiaries all the time. They even offer partial pay and partial points at some hotels. I had to drive a car across the country recently, so I utilized my rewards points. Out of seven nights, I was able to get two nights for $50 plus some points, two nights free, and the rest at a reasonable rate. They were consistent across the board with clean rooms and excellent breakfast.

In essence, what are my choices for hotels? The biggest thing to consider would be the Hilton versus Hampton Inn types of hotels.

When it comes to this, the definitive factor comes down to parking and bellhops. If there's a fee to park, then everything is going to cost you money, and there will be people to tip along the way. In addition to the expense of the room, you will have expensive meals at their restaurant, bell boys, and parking attendants to tip as well as other amenities to purchase. The advantages to these hotels are you don't have to bring any food, water, or snacks with you. There is usually a nice restaurant in the hotel as well and lobbies to relax in, whether working or not. If you want to have a clean, comfortable room without the cost of the frills, Hampton Inn is the way to go.

Since they are both related to an excellent honors program, you know you are getting consistency, and they are top of the line in each category.

Use this link to check it out, and sign-up for their honors program. http://hhonors3.hilton.com/en/index.html

Chapter 7 - Oh To Rest My Weary Head

For the frequent traveler, you will be glad you did. When you let a hotel know that you frequent them and are in their honors program, when available, they will give you free upgrades, and possible amenities like free tickets to something around town. At my last Hampton stay, the observant clerk who checked me in noticed I was looking at the horse racing pamphlet, so he gave me two tickets for free entry to the park.

Get additional tips about the best hotels and hotel rooms in **VIP Bonus Travel Tips** at www.HowToTravelFiveStar.com.

CHAPTER 8

To Uber or not to Uber

"Try not to become a man (person) of success, but rather try to become a man (person) of value."

- Albert Einstein

This is going to be a short chapter on a controversial subject. To Uber or not to Uber. Most big cities have Uber. In my ever so humble opinion, a big city is the safest place to try out an Uber. The horror stories that are around about Uber seem to be about the same in frequency as the airplane accident. Things do happen, but it's very rare. According to the article "Concerns Arise Over Safety of Uber Versus Taxi Rides," from *Claims Journal,* "The taxi industry, facing an existential threat from Uber, has highlighted a series of incidents as evidence that an Uber trip is a gamble passengers should not take. Then again, taxi drivers have assaulted customers, too."[4] The article also pointed out that there is no analyzed statistical data on this. However, there have always been shady issues, perhaps robbery and other criminal activity in taxicabs. The taxi is no more, or less, safe than an Uber.

The more important thing to consider is how it feels for you to get into a car with a total stranger who takes you to a place you're not familiar with. London was having a big problem with this, to the point that if you were anywhere in a pub, or any place at night, in fact, especially if you were a woman, someone would appear and bring what looked like a business card to you. You take it, no big deal. You're the tourist. Upon further inspection, you find it is a fold-open thing that opens up into a small brochure. Very clever. I thought I'd see some tourist coupon of sorts. Instead, there were warnings *do not get in the wrong car*. That might not even be a cab you're getting into. Can you imagine? Women were getting

---

[4] @cjournal. "Concerns Arise Over Safety of Uber Versus Taxi Rides." *Claims Journal*. 29 Feb. 2016. Web. <http://www.claimsjournal.com/news/national/2016/03/01/269134.htm>

Chapter 8 - To Uber Or Not To Uber

into unlicensed cars with unlicensed drivers without even knowing it. Trust your gut, learn to feel your instincts, and as you put your new tools into use, you too will develop your own travel wings.

Before I start on the service, expense, and safety of the Uber, I must relay my best Uber story ever. I was out in Hollywood with a girlfriend. We were off to see her husband play in his band. This was at the House of Blues just weeks before they closed it down in Los Angeles for good. We were having an excellent time. You would think the end of the night cab home would be a bit solemn as the evening was coming to a close. Not with my Uber driver that night. He was on his game and was going to make my Uber ride a private party. When we got in the car, he started to play some dance party music, and then kicked up a cab full of disco lights. The car was filled with colorful spheres of light going 'round and 'round, which was topped off with an actual mini disco ball that sat on the middle console for our entertainment pleasure. And a pleasure it was.

After that wonderful experience, I've since asked every driver where their disco ball is and shared that story with them. That was the most fun I ever had going home in my life!

VIP Guide for the Frequent Flyer

No matter where you go in life, or who you interact with, there is always a rotten apple. That doesn't mean they have to spoil the whole bunch. I have only had two unpleasant incidents with Ubers. On one occasion, I was in Los Angeles. However, I was about eight minutes from Hollywood "off the beaten path." When we used the Uber app, the Uber kept saying they were eight minutes away. Every few minutes, that eight turned into twelve minutes, and back and forth, and so on.

After twenty minutes, I realized we were too far out of the "zone," and the Ubers were taking calls one minute from where they were and not coming to get us. We had no choice but to hail, and hop into, a cab. This is the only instance where a taxi worked out better. Just know this about Uber. If you are not right in the hub of the hustle and bustle, they aren't coming for you.

In another instance, my usual Uber driver was not available, so I went with someone else. I happened to leave my phone in the car. Most drivers would bring an item back to you, especially if they dropped you off at your house. This particular driver took advantage of the situation; he said he wanted me

Chapter 8 - To Uber Or Not To Uber

to place an order for the Uber to come back or pay him cash for my phone. This is not typical behavior for a driver to extort their customers. In fact, more drivers than not are so happy to be driving for you, they remind you that the tip is included in the fare, and you don't have to tip them. I find this to be very refreshing (I tip them anyway).

Other than those two occasions, I believe Uber to be priced better than a taxi, and it is first class service all the way, no matter what level of service you choose. There are different types of service all at different prices, but even their least expensive class of service remains very classy. The cars have regulations as far as the look and cleanliness, and most drivers are dressed in business attire or business casual.

Below is a chart of Ubers in Los Angeles comparing the different services. I usually start with UberX. Sometimes this class of service can cause you to have to wait because there are fewer cars in this class of service. If I want something right away, I usually go with UberXL. Classy service all the way. Just download the app, and you never have to reach for your wallet.

Uber Service	Base Fare	Time Cost (/min)	Distance Cost (/mile)	Minimum Fare	Cancellation Fee
UberX	$0.00	$0.18	$1.00	$4.65	$5.00
UberXL	$3.00	$0.35	$1.85	$7.65	$5.00
UberSelect	$5.00	$0.40	$2.35	$10.65	$5.00
UberBlack	$8.00	$0.45	$3.55	$15.00	$10.00
UberSUV	$15.00	$0.55	$4.25	$25.00	$10.00
UberLUX	$20.00	$0.60	$5.00	$35.00	$10.00

(https://techboomers.com/t/uberx-uberselect-ubertaxi-uberblack)

BOTTOM LINE

Is Uber as unsafe as some may claim? In my opinion, there is far too much hype on the subject, more-so than actual incidents that occur. Criminal activity can occur anywhere, and could just as well happen on the walk back to your hotel since you were too afraid to get into that Uber. Uber has always been at odds with the taxi companies for "taking away" business from them. In that respect, they will always get bad press.

The only way to dispel the rumors is to try it yourself, or keep using it if you already do. It's a wonderful way to travel around any big city in five-star fashion for a three-star price.

If the places you're going are around your hotel, but not in walking distance, it's going to be more

Chapter 8 - To Uber Or Not To Uber

efficient and effective to leave your car parked at the hotel and Uber around the city. Perhaps you can save on a car rental altogether by simply using Uber. If your hotel has a free shuttle to and from the airport, then you are in a better position. If you have to take an Uber to and from the airport, share some rides with fellow business travelers. Not having a car rental and hotel parking fees can save your company a lot in the expense account, and you can justify spending more money on your flight.

In summary, the value versus benefit ratio of using Uber as part of your business travel plan will put you in the red on your travel expense and be an impressive way to tote clients (and yourself) around as well.

Still not certain about the best mode of transportation once you are on the ground? Don't forget to access your copy of **VIP Bonus Travel Tips** by visiting www.HowToTravelFiveStar.com for more information about getting around town.

CHAPTER 9

Jet Setting

*"Management is doing things right;
leadership is doing the right things."*

- Peter Drucker

I had the opportunity to take a private jet a couple of times when I was working on television commercials. Talk about a time saver and a luxury ride.

We were on the way to Telluride, Colorado and Flagstaff, Arizona for a car commercial. Sometimes they all seem to blend, so I can't remember which car brand it was specifically. Probably Toyota, because of its superb handling in extreme weather (now I sound like a commercial). Whichever automotive client it was, they got their wish of severe weather.

VIP Guide for the Frequent Flyer

Our plan to shoot in Flagstaff first was trumped when one of the worst snowstorms ever to face Flagstaff was upon us. That's not when we took the Learjet. We were forced to plow our way through the snow making our pathway on the freeways and side streets. It was quite comical being at the mercy of Bobby Unser Jr. (the race car driver) who was hired as the stunt driver for the picture car. (Let's call it Toyota for the purpose of this story.) We all had to stop and buy chains, and caravan our cars, equipment trucks, the truck hauling the "picture car," vans, and all.

For some reason, the men insisted we put chains on all four of our all-wheel drive vehicle. They bought chains for all four tires of all the vehicles. I'm a woman, and even I know that's not necessary. The typical six-hour drive took us somewhere around nine hours, and we traveled thirty miles per hour on pure white highways. It was one of the most beautiful and scary moments I have ever experienced.

So when does the Learjet come in? We will get to that.

Chapter 9 - Jet Setting

First, let's dispel some myths associated with private chartering. True or false:

1) There are no affordable ways to private charter.
2) Corporate jets are not as safe as commercial airlines.

I won't make you flip the book upside down to read false. Both are false.

Statistically speaking, chances of being killed in any kind of aircraft is 1 in 7,178 in a lifetime vs. a car which is 1 in 98 in a lifetime.[5] It's just our perception that makes things seem so much safer in a car. Car accidents happen every day, but due to the smaller number of people killed or injured and that it is spread out over time, makes it appear safer. When a plane crashes it seems so much more catastrophic because so many people are killed at once. However, if you get into some reading on the truth behind it all, you will see more clearly on the matter.

---

[5] "Is Air Travel Safer Than Car Travel?" *USA Today*. Gannett. Web. <http://traveltips.usatoday.com/air-travel-safer-car-travel-1581.html>

Way back during my previous story, chartering a flight was very expensive. It still is today, depending on exactly what you want, and where you are going. However, there are private corporate jets that are affordable that offer the same amenities. There are two private jet companies that I have discovered that are nothing short of fantastic.

Let's talk about one of my favorite private corporate jet companies I've found thus far. It's called JetSuite. This company is highly rated for safety and comfort.

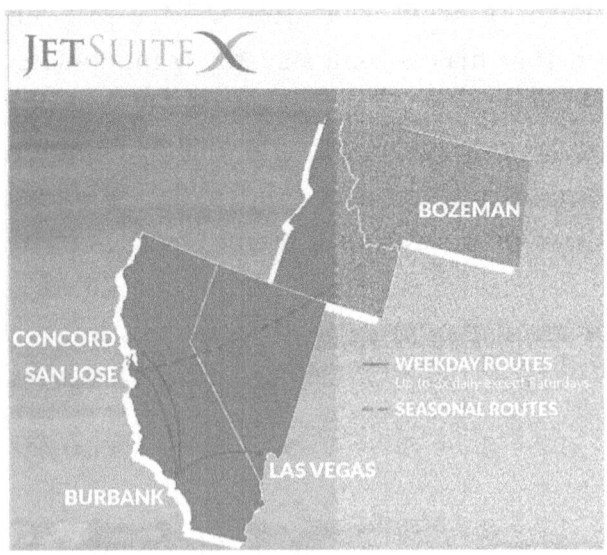

(www.jetsuite.com)

Chapter 9 - Jet Setting

As you can see, this is mainly California-based. However, they have one-way flights on a regular basis as low as one hundred twenty-nine dollars each way. That's competitive with the commercial airlines. The perks are worth every penny. You pull right up to the aviation hangar and park. There are no security lines, no long walks or bus rides to the terminal. This alone saves you so much time, and it relieves the stress of being late. Check with your private jet carrier, but I would say that arriving within thirty minutes of the flight is plenty of time.

There is another private jet company that has a monthly fee for unlimited flights throughout California and Las Vegas. This company is called Surf Air. The monthly fee starts at just $1,950, and the number of flights is unlimited. Can you imagine the amount of time and money you will save if you fly through these areas for your business frequently? It's a no-brainer. Not to mention, you don't have to fight commuters trying to get through the airport.

Finally, there is another secret that is not limited to California. There are flights that the general public has access to. These are private charter jets with "empty leg flights."

These are private jets that flew one way, but are empty for the way back to their base. These are flights that would rather get some money to get back to their base than to fly back empty. These flights get placed on a website, and you can get access to flying privately for a fraction of what booking a private jet would be--sometimes for the cost of a coach ticket. Some empty leg flights are booked per person, and others give great flat fees, so you can get a bunch of corporate travelers to split the cost. For example, there was an empty leg charter jet from San Francisco to Los Angeles. The whole plane was available for $549! So, if you were the solo traveler, that would still rate as an excellent deal, but split between a couple of people, well, you do the math on that. I think the bean counters at the corporation would be happy with your choice.

Think outside the box and learn about more unique ways to travel in **VIP Bonus Travel Tips** by visiting www.HowToTravelFiveStar.com.

CHAPTER 10

Final Thoughts

Whether traveling for work or play, enjoying the journey should absolutely be as much fun as the destination. If you are traveling for a job, then the journey should be more fun than the destination! The people you meet along the way, the stories you can hear and tell will open doors into special moments in time that will stay with you forever. Take a chance on *You Air* - Believe in yourself; you can make the most of your journey!

People make all the difference, and that includes you. If you are polite and kind to those who are helping you take your journey, you will get far better results than those who put up a fuss or are rude to anyone in any service along the way.

VIP Guide for the Frequent Flyer

People you meet along the way in the airport, on the plane, at the hotel, these people can touch your life, and your heart, with a short funny exchange, or an enlightening "ah ha" gift of knowledge that they are willing to share. So remember, kept an open mind and an open heart to those around you. You never know who they might be, what stories they have, and how they might be able to help you. This is the priceless part of traveling, and when you travel with less stress. It keeps you open to receiving the messages the universe may have in store for you.

As I said in the beginning, I would love for this book to be interactive. I have more stories to write, and yours might be one of them if you share a great experience or some helpful information regarding your corporate travel experiences.

Get your FREE VIP Bonus Travel Tips:
www.HowToTravelFiveStar.com

Share with us on Facebook:
www.facebook.com/traveltvshow

HAPPY TRAILS!

Keep an eye out for my next series in travel, which will explore specific destinations, and dive into International Travel.

About The Author

Gina Dagostino spent ten years in television production, both as a Production Manager and a Producer. While managing everything from million dollar budgets for BMW commercials to music videos, she was also rallying and arranging transportation for creatures great and small - from 'A' list superstars to wide-mouthed alligators. Whether roaming the planet on puddle jumpers in Belize to private jets in Colorado, she has acquired a multitude of tricks and tips from around the globe - and she wants to share them with you.

Gina consults with corporations, both large and small, to make their business travelers more productive by keeping their travel experience comfortable and stress-free. A proud member of International Living, and ITWPA (The International Travel Writers & Photographer's Alliance), she spends her time sharing the knowledge she has acquired first-hand with corporations to help them meet their budgetary bottom line, while ensuring their employees' and consultants' bottoms are comfortable along their journey.

Always a humanitarian, Gina started a charity after the 2003 Old Fire ravished through the mountain communities of Lake Arrowhead, in southern California. The charity raised enough money to get an entire community back on their feet.

During her free time, Gina loves to travel for pleasure. Her favorite place to travel to and write about is Ireland. She has traveled to Ireland multiple times and loves the culture, vibe, and people. To learn more about Ireland

About the Author

and Gina's travels, visit irishchatroom.net and emeraldisletreasurechest.com.

www.ingramcontent.com/pod-product-compliance
Lightning Source LLC
Chambersburg PA
CBHW060359190526
45169CB00002B/668